The Victim Survived

~My testimony~

RHONDA TAYLOR

ISBN: 1974020266
ISBN-13: 978-1974020263

CONTENTS

DEDICATION

I would like to thank God my Father and the Healer of minds. I thank God for putting my life back together again. Without him this book would not have been written. God said to me, "Daughter, others that can't see you need to hear from you." He said, "Tell them, teach them, and lead them to me. When they hear what I did for you they will search for me also."

I thank my mother and father who taught me about God and how to love Him. I thank God for my son and my two daughters who have been my backbone and my strength. They are some praying youth.

I thank God for the great leaders he has placed in my life. Pastor Harold Patton who led me to salvation. Bishop T.D. Jakes for his Broken, Battered Women's Ministry. Vernon Thompson, a great teacher whom God appointed to teach and ordain me. My spiritual mom, Pastor Gladys Wofford. Bishop David E. Martin, a great teacher and a great leader.

I also need to reserve special mention and thanks for Prophet Kevin Etta and Pastor Immaculata Etta who have been mentors, spiritual counselors and guides to me. They've believed in me, encouraged and propelled me to fulfill my destiny. God bless you all.

1
WHEN I WAS A CHILD

I grew up in a home with a large family. I'm the youngest of seven children. There are four girls and three boys. My oldest sister and brother left home early. So, it was just my mom and dad, myself, two sisters and two brothers.

When my mother and father would go to work, my next-to-the-oldest sister would keep me, and -- gosh, did they have a time when Mom and Dad left! They would sneak boys into the house. One sister was trying to teach the other sister how to kiss a boy. She would run out of the house and when they caught her they brought her back and tried to teach her again. By the time they figured mom and dad would return home they would put the boys out of the house.

I didn't tell at that time. I was just five years old. My mom and dad worked very hard to take care of us. They kept us in church all week long and on Sundays. My mother even kept her grandchildren, trying to keep them from being hurt in their own homes. She would sometimes send me to their homes to watch out for them so I could come back and tell her what happened.

I witnessed my oldest sister being abused by her husband and my nephew being molested by his own dad. I was standing at the bathroom door when my sister was asking her husband to let their son come out of the bathroom. When he finally let him go he was naked from the waist down and he had been crying, he was red and swollen. My sister asked, "what did you do to him?" And he said, "I put Vaseline on him." And then he said, "he's okay, go and sit down." I walked away with her. I didn't know what to feel or to say. I was only a child myself.

When I returned home that Sunday I told my mom and dad what happened. My mom cried. But I still didn't understand why? Little did my mom know, but molestation was taking place in our home too. When I was only five years old, my youngest brother would come in my room while everyone was asleep and get me and take me into the living room and molest me.

One night my mother walked in on him and said, "what are you doing to my baby?" He got up, pulled up his pants and left the room. While he was walking out the room she said, "if your daddy knew you were doing this he would kill you." She took me in the girls room then laid me on the bed and checked me to see if I had been tampered with and then said, "if your daddy finds out he will hurt your brother."

At this point I, stayed silent about everything concerning me. I just went to the places my mom would send me to watch out for her grandchildren. I would sometimes miss school to go to my sister's home because my other little niece was being molested in her home as well.

My mom used to keep my little niece all the time and she stayed sick. My mom stayed at Children's Medical Center with her; she had seizures all the time. My mother told the doctors she was being molested at home and they found that to be true. My mother and father went to court and took me with them. They told me they had her grandfather in custody. My niece's mom and her aunt had her in the bathroom and my mom sent me to listen and hear what they were saying.

They told my niece that her grandfather would die in prison if he went and if that happened it would be her fault and the child started to cry. By the time it came for her to testify, she told the judge that he didn't touch her. My mom and my dad both cried because they knew her mom and her aunt had convinced the child to lie to the judge. So my niece continued to go through it all.

Years passed by, and I was about eleven years old when my mom sent me to help my oldest sister out because she had become very ill. I would miss school to help her with her children. I would walk them to school and help her clean the house. I witnessed my sister being abused by her husband. When I went back home I told my mom and dad about all that took place. My poor mother was shaken on account of her grandchildren living in two different places but going through the same things. My mom and dad had their hands full.

I would sometimes go to school and just daydream, because I was so worried about them. One day my teacher asked my mother, "how is your daughter at home? She is very smart but she daydreams a lot." My mother told her she would talk to me and find out what was wrong but she never did, because she had other things on her mind that she was trying to deal with.

I was the little girl who cried to go to church. So one night my mom and dad went to church and when we got there the Bishop called my mother to come up and I went with her. He said, "your baby here is very watchful and curious, and she loves to come to church." He said, "never stop her from coming." He also said, "she worries a lot about her mom and her dad and that's why she daydreams a lot." I don't recall my mother responding to him. She just listened, she never asked me what was wrong.

I have always tried to wear a mask around my mom and dad because they were already going through a lot. I would also watch my dad cry from being mistreated by my brothers that he raised and took care of. My brothers would get drunk or high and come into the house and curse at my dad. They would steal his cars, wreck them and then talk bad to him.

They were so mean to my dad. I told myself that when I got big I would do something about it. I would confide to my next-to-the-oldest sister all my thoughts and feelings. When she left home and moved to Houston, I was so hurt. I felt like I had lost my best friend. My mom would send me to stay with her for the summer and when it was time to return home I'd cry my eyes out, because I knew it was bad at home; always trouble and no peace.

Who could I tell? My oldest sister was going through stuff, the other sister set no good examples for me. She would have intercourse with her boyfriend in the same bed I was sleeping in. There was nowhere and no-one I could turn to. Daddy was at work and Momma was sick; I felt trapped. I told myself that one day I would move out of there.

Shortly after, my oldest sister was so sick that she needed to be cared for. So she moved back in with us. She was not only sick physically, but she was slowly losing her mind. I would be in the car with her and as she was driving she would be in a daze and running red lights. I know God encamped his angels around us. He knew that my sister was not in her right mind and unfit to be driving, so he shielded us from all hurt, harm and danger.

The word of God says in Psalm 34:7, "The angel of the Lord encamps around those who fear him, and he delivers them." The word of God also tells us in Psalm 121:7-8, "The Lord shall preserve them from all evil: he shall preserve thy soul. The Lord shall preserve thy going out and thy coming in from this time forth, and even for evermore." God knew my sister's state of mind and, on account of His purpose, He was not going to let the enemy harm us. I would return home and sometimes I would tell and sometimes I would not.

After a while my sister stopped driving, because she had gotten worse, mentally. So now I had one sister that was mentally ill, another sister that was also ill, a brother and occasionally my parents' grandchildren falling ill. My mom was no longer working due to poor health. My daddy's income was the only income we had in the home. It was very hard for him because he worked two jobs. Sometimes, he would haul trash so that he could salvage scrap iron to sell. I used to go with my dad and watch him work laying bricks, building homes and churches. Sometimes they wouldn't even pay him for his hard work.

I saw my daddy cry sometimes, because it was so hard on him. Shortly after, my mom fell ill again, this time mentally. My daddy said, "Something is not right with your mom." I knew it, because when my dad would leave for work my mom would take out pictures of loved ones that were deceased and light candles and make me stand there with her. I would watch the pictures and I was told not to move. I told daddy what she was doing while he was away.

One night she went out in the backyard and started digging a hole. Every night about the same time she would make the hole deeper and deeper until it began to look like a grave. Then she put all her purses, pictures, etc. into the hole. It's like she would 'time' my dad to get all this done before he would return home from work.

This particular night my dad returned home from work, relaxed a bit, ate supper and went to bed. While he slept, my mother came into the room to kill him but he awoke and got hold of her. From that time on, he had to sleep with a chair propped behind the door. He tried to scare her by telling her he would send her to Terrell, Texas if she didn't stop what she was doing.

One night my dad returned from work. Mom and I were standing around when he looked up and said, "Sister..." (which was her nickname). He said it again, "Sister... what's wrong baby?" He repeated, "Baby, what's wrong?". Then he grabbed her and hugged her and she began shaking like someone was literally shaking her body. It looked so unreal, her body was shaking so bad that it was shaking my dad as well.

Later my dad took my mom to Pittsburg, Texas to live with her mother who was a praying woman. My grandmother asked my dad to bring her daughter home and she would get well. My grandmother also told my dad that nothing was too hard for God.

Mom stayed there six weeks and we went every weekend to visit her. At first, she didn't recognize us. But as time passed she started to talk to us. She asked us about what happened to her. When Dad eventually brought Mom back home, it wasn't long after that my immediate older sister became ill. One day while daddy was driving, we were sitting in the back seat and my sister had been running a fever off and on. As we were riding along, she started choking and tried to jump out of the car while it was moving. Whatever it was that came over her that day tried to kill her. She was gasping for air.

I was so scared and I kept saying, "Daddy look at her! She's trying to jump out of the car!" Dad said, "Don't let her jump out!" When he pulled the car over, my mom jumped out first then my dad. My sister was pulling this thick slime out of her throat, almost as long as her arm. My mom and dad took her to church, the Bishop prayed for her and the demons left her body.

As a little girl I never understood what my dad meant when he said she was either demon possessed or a victim of witchcraft. I only knew it was very scary. The bible speaks about demons. In the narrative of Matthew 17:17-20, Jesus heals a demon possessed boy. The Bible describes a scene where they come into the crowd a man approaches Jesus and kneels before him saying, "Lord have mercy on my son, he has seizures and is suffering greatly; he often falls into the fire or into the water. I brought him to your disciples and they could not heal him." Jesus rebuked the demon and it came out of the boy. He was healed that very instant.

In Mark 1:23-26, a man in the synagogue who was possessed by an evil spirit cried out, "What do you want with us, Jesus of Nazareth? Have you come to destroy us?" Jesus said, "Be quiet, and come out of him!" The evil spirit shook the man violently and then came out of him.

In Matthew 17:17-20, the disciples were unable to drive out this demon and they asked Jesus why. He pointed out to them their lack of faith in the power of God.

The power of God to move mountains is activated by faith. Faith as the size of a mustard seed, which is a very small seed. Perhaps the disciples had tried to drive out the demon by their own ability rather than by Gods. Or by their own 'force' versus by faith (and confidence) in the power of God. If you feel weak or powerless as a Christian, you should examine your faith. Make sure you do not trust in your own ability, or even trust in *your* faith -- but in the ability of God. It wasn't that my mom and dad didn't know God, but their faith was in man's ability and not God's -- which is why the demon was running rabid in our home. My parents were faithful in church, even in giving. Sometimes my dad would give all he had to the church in his desire to see God's miraculous intervention in our home.

He was once asked for so many thousands of dollars in order to see my oldest sister healed. My dad sold his car to get the money and my sister became well for a little while. And then she got worse. My parents put their faith in man and not God, because they didn't realize that God has given all believers the authority to cast out demons – including the demons in our home – provided their faith is at work. Shortly after that happened my mom got a call saying her oldest son was in prison. She started to cry and went back to the church. The church folks asked for more money and my dad didn't have it. He was all out.

My mom flew out to Tucson, Arizona to be at court with my brother. Prayer at that time coupled with my mom and dad's faith brought him out. When I saw that I said, "Mom, why is it that you pay for everything? Why do we stand in line to see a prophet? Why do you pay his secretary twenty dollars to see him, mama? Why?" She looked down at me and said, "Don't you say that again or something bad will happen when you talk like that."

As we approached to see the 'prophet', I still didn't understand why. When we arrived, he was sitting in a chair two stairs up as if he were on a throne. My mom kneeled down, but I did not. Then he said to her, "Your little girl is so curious." Then my mom looked at me. I didn't blink, I stared at him thinking, 'Who are you?' And, 'Is this of God?'

Sometimes they would turn off the lights and it would be dark in the church. I never saw anybody reading from the Bible. They had a choir but only prophecy went forth and the taking of money. As a little girl, I couldn't understand it. Everybody seemed okay with it, while I felt like it was wrong but didn't say any more about it. I kept quiet just like I did about everything that was hurting me, because I lived in a 'don't tell' house.

I didn't have a voice to speak, so I literally watched my family suffer one calamity after another. It got so bad at home that my dad met this prophet and he told my dad to leave my mom. Because my parents believed every word he spoke my dad left and moved into his own apartment. One side of me was okay with it, because of what my dad had gone through with my mother's boys and the other side of me felt bad because my mom needed him.

My mother's words were, "I'm hurting, but I trust in the Lord. He will see us through." Then she cried. We got put out of our home. Mom called Dad and told him she needed his help and that we were getting put out of our home. I don't recall my dad responding to her, but just as she had said - - God made a way for us.

My sister came from Houston to visit. She and I went to visit dad and she asked him what happened. Dad told her and she didn't get mad, because she knew that he had gone through a lot. My dad had three children with my mother, but he treated all the children the same -- whether he was their biological father or not. But my brothers abused and disrespected him and my mom didn't want to deal with all the hurt that was being caused by her sons. That was, ultimately, why my dad left.

Note:
Our Father and our Lord, The Great "I AM", The Almighty God said, "I will be a Father to the fatherless."

Psalm 46: 1-4 says, "God is our refuge and strength, an ever-present help in trouble. Therefore we will not fear, though the earth give way and the mountains fall into the heart of the sea, though its waters roar and foam and the mountains quake with their surging. Selah. There is a river whose streams make glad the city of God, the holy place where the Most High dwells."

2
GROWING UP TOO FAST

Proverbs 22:16 says, "Train up a child in the way he should go and when he is old he will not turn from it." Living in the kind of home I was raised in, caused me to be very curious about having a boyfriend. As a young girl about twelve years old, my dad and mom got back together. Our home was the same, if not worse.

One weekend my mom and dad went out of town. My immediate older sister, was accustomed to going out to concerts and clubs. So when my parents would leave, she would call my cousin up on the phone and make plans to go clubbing. My sister told my cousin and her pals that her kid sister (me) was with her, so they decided to take me along.

There I was, twelve years old, in a club being exposed to club life. Shortly after, my sister got pregnant and she was only five years older than me. When she had her baby she still wanted to go to the club and to concerts, so my mother made me keep her little boy. Sometimes I would cry and say to her, "I didn't have him, why are you making me keep her baby?"

My mom replied that since I was not going anywhere, it made sense to keep the baby and let my sister go out. So I did. I had her baby more than she did and, ultimately, felt like I was the baby's mother.

So for all of you young and old mothers that have your children raising their little sisters or brothers or any other little family members while you go out -- and they are themselves underage -- you are causing them to grow up too fast. Let them enjoy their childhood. Don't steal their childhood away from them. I'm speaking based on my own experiences, because as you continue to read this book you'll realize that I had no childhood. It'd been taken away from me.

My mother kept telling me how everyone always depended on her for everything and how she didn't get to enjoy her childhood either – probably why she didn't realize she was doing the same thing to me. The word of God in Ephesians 6:4 says, "Fathers, provoke not your children to wrath; but bring them up in the nurture and admonition of the Lord." Colossians 3:21 says, "Fathers, provoke not your children to anger, lest they be discouraged."

3
TEENAGE PREGNANCY

The days turned into months and the months into years. At the age of fourteen I got pregnant. I would skip school and go to his house. The very first time I was exposed to intercourse, I got pregnant. One night as I lay on the sofa I felt really sick. I said, "Mama, I'm sick to my stomach. It feels like something is crawling in my belly and it won't stop." She said to my dad, "We need to take her to the hospital and find out what's going on with her", and my dad said, "Okay."

On our way, my dad asked my mom what it could be and she said she really couldn't say. Then he looked at me and asked was I okay and I said no. When we arrived at the hospital, me and Mom went in. The doctor asked what was wrong. I said it feels like butterflies are in my belly. When the doctor finished examining me he looked at my mom and said, "Your little girl is pregnant." Then she looked at me and said, "Now I have to find a way to tell your daddy without him getting really upset."

As we are getting into the car Dad asks, "What did the doctor say?" Mom replies: "Wait till we get home." Dad continues: "She better not be pregnant." Mom tries to change the subject: "She is craving fish, please stop and get some for her." But my dad is persistent: "What's wrong with her?

When Mom finally said the words, "She's pregnant" my dad turned and looked at me. I said to myself, 'I'm really in for it now', because the sound of my dad's angry voice alone would scare you and make you cry. "Pregnant!" I said, "Yes sir." He said, "You are a baby and you're having a baby." Then he said, "It's okay, baby girl. I'm not mad at you. Disappointed? Yes. But it's okay. We'll get through this. I still love you, but the facts remain the same." My dad did not like the guy that I was with. He said to me, "Baby girl, he is not good for you. He drinks real heavy. Drinks and he gets high. I don't like him for you. He's only going to do you bad and not good." I said, "Daddy he will not. "Don't worry. It's okay."

I went back to school after having a 6lbs 8oz baby girl, a bundle of joy. I made promises to her. I told her, "Not only are you my daughter, but you are also my doll. I will not let anyone harm you." A short while later, both her dad and me dropped out of school. I got a job and continued to go to modeling school that my dad had been paying for and was continuing to pay. Two months later I stopped going to modeling school, too. My dad got really upset at me and said, "Baby girl, you're throwing your life away." I couldn't see it at the time and I started staying away from home.

I continued to go with my boyfriend and stayed at his mom's house some nights. My parents were so upset at me and his family for allowing me to be there underage. Little did my dad know I'd told my boyfriend's mom that he had put me out just so he could get me out of the house. I said to my boyfriend, "I have a baby now… I'm grown. I can do what I want." I told him that I'd been trying to find a way out of the house, that I'd been going through some things at home and having a child was my way out. He saw things my way. All the while I was hoping his mom would never ask my dad about that, because it wasn't true. I just wanted out.

In Matthew 23:37, it says: "O Jerusalem, Jerusalem. How often I have longed to gather your children together, as a hen gathers her chicks under her wings, but you were not willing." Jesus knows better than anyone the pain of being hurt by those he loved. He is able to share our pain and disappointment and give grace to bear them.

As a young girl, I'd told myself several times that whenever I get the chance I would leave home. It was so much pain at home with my family and I'd been exposed to so many things. My prayer to the readers of this book is that you will take your children up in your arms and tell them that you love them and tell them what they can become so that no one else can give them a name. Don't let the streets school your baby. Admonish them, teach them, lead them and guide them.

God said don't allow the enemy to steal your children from you. He said children let us know the world continues. Tell your children about God and then live the life that you talk about. God said I'm holding you responsible for how you raise your children. In Isaiah 54:13, it says: "All thy children shall be taught by the Lord, and great will be your children's peace."

The word of God also says in Proverbs 22:6, "Train a child in the way he should go, and when he is old he will not depart from it." When you train someone, you spend time with them. We must take the time with our youth, teach them to love and respect themselves; and most of all to love God.

4

AN ABUSIVE HOME

It happened so fast like I was dreaming. Now me and my boyfriend have moved out our parents' home. We got our first apartment, just us three: me, my little girl and my boyfriend. He and I both worked, but he only worked on days that I did not work on. I worked full-time and his sister would baby-sit for us. However, it wasn't long before my boyfriend lost his job so he stayed home while I worked. Then we switched again when I found out I was pregnant for the second time. I was only sixteen years old and he was nineteen.

He went to work with my brother and I really dreaded that. His drinking got heavier and it became a problem. My family found out that I was pregnant again. They called me from out of town and asked, "What do you plan to do with this baby?" And I said, "Have it." My brother then said, "If you do, we will not have anything else to do with you", and – boy, did that hurt! When he said that I hung up on him.

My sister called me back and said, "Baby sis, you don't have to go through that if you don't want to." I said, "I am having my baby." About a week later my boyfriend started to get drunk and saying things like, "Have you been looking out the window at men?" I asked him, "What's wrong?" and overlooked that incident.

The following week he got drunk again and said, "Don't you even think about leaving?" He said if I did he would hurt me, then I became afraid of him. I was only 110lbs and he was wearing a 42-44 pants size can you even picture that! Now he had placed fear into my heart so every time I thought about leaving I was too afraid. Then he made a bat with screws in it. At that point I didn't know what was going through his mind. All I knew was he was crazy enough to use it on me if I thought about leaving him.

One morning as I lay in my bed, everything was going through my mind: the fear of leaving and the fear of staying and being pregnant. So I said first things first: I called my sister and her husband and told them that I am ready to go through with the abortion. They gave me the money for it and two days later I asked my dad to drop me off and come back later to pick me up. I told him I would call him when I was ready.

As I went into the clinic, I saw all these beds lined up waiting for the women as they came in. They took me to this room where I started to become really afraid, but the nurses said for me to relax. There was a nurse on each side of the bed and one at my feet who was coaching me on what to do next. They hooked this thing up and it looked like a vacuum cleaner with a lot of buttons and there was a peak hole where I could see the baby go through it. It was so painful that I felt like I was dying. That's the worst thing a woman could ever endure. I cried so hard and then I saw my baby going through a hole then into the trash, that's horrible!

After it happened I said to myself, 'How could people be so cruel, even the nurses? How can you stand there and hook an object up to a woman's body and dispose of a baby into the garbage?' I had such a hard time mentally after that. I told my boyfriend that I had a miscarriage while he was at work, and he didn't seem to care at all. I kept rehearsing over and over in my mind what happened and tasking myself with thoughts of why I had done that.

I didn't know to repent. I just cried. My body was still trying to heal from all of that. My boyfriend was so obsessed with sex that he didn't care if I was sick. He would force himself on me and when I would say no, he would even hold me down with both wrist together and force himself on me. Sometimes I would just cry and he would use any type of objects on me before and after he was done. He was so mean to me.

I would think to myself, 'What is going through his mind when he does that to me?' He would tell me when he was finished that no man will want me and I better not leave.

I was so afraid of him and he knew it. I wouldn't even tell my family about the things he was doing to me. If my daddy knew what he was doing he would have killed him, so I stayed and he repeatedly got drunk and took advantage of me. He would get up the next morning just like nothing ever happened and I would forgive him.

One night he got so drunk, our little girl was watching him stumble over things and throw things through the house. He got up out of a chair, went into the kitchen and got a jug of water and began throwing it on me repeatedly. The third time he came back, I pretended like I couldn't breath and he stopped and ran back into the kitchen. I got my baby in my arms and ran out the door. I didn't stop running until I got to my sister's doorstep.

I said, "Please let me in, he's after me, he's going to hurt me real bad." I looked back and saw him running really fast with that bat in his hand. My sister slammed the door in his face and he beat her door repeatedly with the bat until she said, "Girl, you and your baby have to go." By the time she opened the door he accidentally hit her with the bat across her hand and it cut her hand really bad. Then he came to where I was. I was holding my baby tight because I was so scared. He said, "You want out?" and I said no, out of fear. Then he said, "You got it!"

He threw the keys down and they hit the baby and when I started crying he ran out the door. My sister's hand was messed up. When I left her house, the guy living upstairs said to me, "One day he's going to kill you. Next time he comes after you, run to my house -- I got something for him." But I said, "No, I can't." The guy upstairs liked me for himself, but I was too afraid to talk to anybody because I feared for my life.

That night I went back to my sister's home and fell asleep on her sofa with my baby lying on top of me. She said you cannot stay here and I told her I was going back home. Two years later I got pregnant by him again, things seemed to have gotten better. Fear will make you do things that you don't want to do.

My boyfriend had my mind so wrapped up in him that everything he said I believed it. He said things like you can't leave, you're not pretty, but this other girl I know is so fine, but not you. I believed him because my self-esteem was so low.

That's what Satan wants, is your mind. God said, "For I am the Lord, your God, who takes hold of your right hand and says to you, Do not fear; I will help you. Do not be afraid." (Isaiah 41:13).

"But whosoever listens to me will live in safety and be at ease, without fear of harm." (Proverbs 1:33).

"Do not be afraid of those who kill the body but cannot kill the soul. Rather, be afraid of the One who can destroy both soul and body in hell." (Matthew 10:28).

"For God did not give us a spirit of fear, but a spirit of power, of love and of a sound mind." (II Timothy 1:7).

5
SCARED STRAIGHT

Things were looking a little better. He still drank, but was a little quieter now. This time I started to feel real sick when the doctor said, "Mrs. Smith you are three months pregnant." I said, "This time I am having my baby" and when I told the child's father, he didn't say a word. It seemed as if when he heard the word, "baby", that was his license to act up again. He started getting drunk again; he would shove me when he got angry and when he got mad at his family he would take it out on me. I said, "Oh Lord! Here we go again." Fear has come back to haunt me. I asked him, "What's wrong? Why are you doing this to me?" He would only get worse.

During my time of labor my dad had to be there with me while my boyfriend was at home drunk under the table. Each time I was giving birth to our babies he wasn't there. My dad was there holding my hand through it all. I had a 7lb 8oz baby girl, a beautiful little girl. I told my boyfriend if he keep on hurting me I would not keep on having babies for him and he said let's get married. Six weeks after our second little girl was born we got married. I was eighteen years old.

That same night we got married, we were riding in the car with his aunt and he said, "Let's get out of the car; we'll walk the rest of the way." I said to myself, 'I know he's not telling her this.' His aunt asked him why, since we were only four blocks away from home. He said it didn't matter and she should let us out, so she stopped the car and we got out. I asked him, "Why did you do that?" and he said, "I need to talk to you before we get to the house with everybody else." Then I said, "Okay."

He said, "I want you to know that I only married you to make your daddy mad. I don't love you like that. I only wanted to prove to your family that I could have you; I liked you, wanted you and there was nothing they could do about it." I said, "You went through all of this to prove my Daddy wrong?" And he said, "Yes... and I don't need you to keep talking to me about it."

At that point, it seemed like the wires in my brain became crossed. I felt like I had just signed my life over to Satan and I cried all the way home and he was smiling. When we arrived at his family's home everybody was there waiting, his family alone -- my dad had said to me, "This is one wedding I'm not attending." So none of my family was there, just my two girls.

That night he got drunk. But nothing happened. He fell asleep. A few months later we moved into our new place with our two girls. My dad would come and get them and take them to my mom's house so I could go to work. My husband and I worked together with his dad. He told me that he was being exposed to street women, or I should say, "women of the night."

We were doing well for about two years straight. He still got drunk but he would just fall asleep afterwards. I guess I bragged a little too soon. He wanted to experiment on me during intimacy and when I wouldn't let him he would hold me down and thrust into me so hard and fast. I would have flash backs. And just when I would think it's over, it would happen again. And again and again... abuse after abuse after abuse.

One morning I said to him, "I can't take this anymore." And he said, "Take what?" and continued washing out the bathtub. He asked me what I was talking about. I said, "Every time you drink you turn into someone else and I'm tired of it." He didn't say anything, he just looked straight ahead like he was not listening.

Our daughters were in the living room watching television when he jumped up and said, "Do you want out of the marriage?" and I said, "Yes." Then he got silent again. I then ran into the living room with my babies because I knew he was up to something. I got them and stood by the kitchen, then he ran in to where we were and started throwing things through the house. I hid my babies behind the sofa.

They watched their daddy throw furniture across the room. When he looked over at them and saw how scared they were of him he stopped and went for a walk. All three of us were scared straight. He was out of control.

When he came back inside he said, "Baby, please don't leave me. I can't make it without you and my kids... please don't leave. I can't make it without you. I will go crazy if you leave me." He kept saying, "I'm sorry, I'm sorry." Everything in me wanted to believe him. I did. I stayed with my husband.

We ended up moving again, because he lost his job and we didn't have enough income to pay the rent and other bills. So we moved into a cheaper but larger apartment. This time we let his sister live with us and sometimes her boyfriend. Our apartment was based on income. I didn't work but my husband worked a part-time job in construction.

After sitting at home for a couple of months, all kind of thoughts began to race through my mind about how my husband had been abusing me, how he wasn't there while I was giving birth to our little girls, how my dad kept on telling me I will get tired soon and he hoped before it was too late and how he said I had just given up my life to have nothing. My dad would ask me, "What's wrong with you baby girl?" He kept saying something is so wrong with this picture and one day you will figure out what. You'll ask yourself why you took all this and stayed with this man. He said, "I'm praying for you that God will bring you out."

One night while everyone was asleep, my sister-in-law had her boyfriend over. That particular night my husband slept in the living room and my girls and I slept in our room. My sister-in-law's boyfriend walked from their room to the bathroom naked. He knew my bedroom door was open. The next morning I waited until my husband went to work and I told his sister what happened the previous night and how her boyfriend disrespected our home. She said okay, she would talk to him.

When my husband got home, I told him what had happened and he talked to his sister about it. She asked him why I didn't tell him about it first, and said that should tell him something about me. His sister tried to flip it back on me and told my husband she didn't like me anyway. My husband told her to get out but she kept on protesting her boyfriend's innocence and said it was his wife (me) that was lying. He told her to get her stuff and get out of his house. She said nothing with us will last. As she was getting her things I remained quiet. Little did I know she left something in my house for me.

A month after she left I became really ill. My vision was bad. I began hearing voices in my house. I would walk through the house and scream and talk to myself. The lady who lived downstairs under me would take her broom and hit the ceiling in order for me to shut up, and I would not until it was time for my husband to come home then the voices would leave. I wouldn't even tell him what was happening to me. One day he came home from work. I had thought about all of the things he had done to me. I had two wire hangers wrapped around both of my hands and when he came in he asked, "Why are you looking that way?" I said, "Why do you want to know?" He asked what was wrong with me.

I jumped up off the bed and began hitting him with the wire hangers that were wrapped around my hands. He tried to push me down but I jumped right back up and continued striking at him. Finally, I stopped and he grabbed me and said, "What's wrong?" I started to cry and said, "I'm tired of a lot of things." He said, "What things?" But I never said.

The next day he left for work and the same illness hit me again. I made my way to a pay phone to call my dad. I was crying and I said, "Daddy I'm so sick." And he said, "What's wrong?" I told him I was having bad headaches and he came and got my things. While he was moving my things he raised my bed up off the floor and there was a dead plant under my bed right in the center. My dad asked, "What in the world is this dead plant doing here?" And I said, "Daddy, that was my husband's sister's plant that she had in her window." My dad said, "This is witchcraft, the same thing that was done to your older sister when she almost died." He said, "Stay away from that family."

I moved in with my mom and dad and the headaches got worse. My dad took me to the emergency room and they ran tests on me and found nothing. My dad said, "It's prayer time." I had to keep real still and quiet so that I would not feel the pain from the headaches. One month later, I found out I was pregnant. This time my husband was happy, because he thought that meant we were going to be together again. But it didn't happen. I stayed with my parents. When the time came, I had a 8lb 9oz baby boy. So handsome he could have passed for a little girl.

We must come to realize that Satan puts fear in our lives so that we will not become all that God created us to be. He uses individuals to deposit bad things into our lives so that we can doubt God.

Sometimes we bring things on our own selves by being disobedient to God and to our parents; even though I went through some things as a child -- and yes it plays a major role in your life when you are exposed -- but when you get exposed to positive things then it becomes a choice. It's sad to say that I was surrounded by all negative things in my life, so my choice was to do what I wanted to do and live how I wanted to live, not thinking about the setbacks that would follow.

Now I'm fearful and in despair. Who can help me? Everybody I know is doing worse than I am or the same. Who can help me? Who can I talk to about what I'm going through without them broadcasting my business all over? Who can I tell that I'm struggling with all these different demons without them thinking I'm crazy or saying, "She brought this on herself", etc. Who can I tell that I'm in a marriage and I'm scared straight? Who can I tell that this man has stripped away my self-esteem? Who can I tell that this man threatened that if I leave him he will do something to me? Who can I tell without it going to the streets and to the churches? When I tell the church they tell other churches. So, who can I tell?

Once again I am silent, just like when I was as a child. Don't tell. But God heard me and brought me out of harm's way. He afflicted the enemy that was trying to hurt me. He silenced my accuser.

Psalm 46:1-3 says, "God is our refuge and strength, an ever-present help in trouble. Therefore we will not fear, though the earth be removed; and though the mountains be carried into the midst of the sea; though the waters thereof roar and be troubled; though the mountains shake with swelling thereof."

Psalm 138:7, "Though I walk in the midst of trouble, thou wilt preserve my life; you stretch out your hand against the anger of my foes, with your right hand you save me."

Matthew 11:28 lets us know God will give us rest.

6
BROKEN DREAMS

Now that I'm free from the abuser what next? I started my new job and was really enjoying life. After work I would return home to my three babies, my mom and my dad. My mom kept the kids while I worked. It seemed just too good to be true. Every now and then my husband would come by the house to see the kids and me, but I didn't want any part of it. So during his visit with the children, I would go outside or into another room away from him.

The visits started fading away little by little. About two months later, as I got off work (I worked from 11:00 p.m. to 7:00 a.m.), I came home and my mother asked me if I had heard anything from my husband. I said no, not in about two months. She said his daddy came by looking for him and that he had been missing for days.

The next day I went to work and when I returned home my mom said, "Your husband came by last night." Mom told me that something appeared to be seriously wrong with him. She knew him to be a very, very clean man but he looked disheveled, without sleep and his clothes were filthy. He had said that he'd come to see me. Mom said that he'd told her, "I'm sorry for all the things I'd done to your daughter and how I took advantage of her all the time. I abused her real bad, time after time. Ma'am, I'm sorry." And then he left.

My mother said to me, "If I didn't love God, I would have done something to him for telling me how he had abused you and how he went

22

into details about it." I couldn't believe some of the things he had said. God made him confess. My mom and dad never knew. They had a feeling something was going on -- but not that! When she told me those things I began to cry. She said, "I knew he was hurting you, but God made him confess to me -- all the things he has done to you. Little did she know, that still wasn't all.

Two days later my brother-in-law came and told me they found him downtown having a seizure and they had to rush him to the hospital. He had a nervous breakdown. My brother-in-law said they took him to the psychiatric ward and when the doctor asked him what caused him to be in the shape that he was in, he said, "I want my wife and children back in my life. She left me." When I heard that, one side of me felt bad but the other side didn't. I was too afraid to trust him again.

When I got ready to go see him my brother-in-law said, "Don't go out there... the family is mad at you and they are blaming you for his illness." When he said that I began to cry and I told him, "Your brother abused me and I did nothing." He said he knew and continued to say, "Don't go out there... the doctors will not let you see him." My dad said, "Didn't I tell you about that family? Why don't you listen to me?"

About a week later my husband asked to see us, so they had no choice but to let us see him. Me and the kids went. He would know who we are one minute, and the next start asking who we are. That hurt me so bad but I still didn't like to see him like that. I didn't want my kids to see their daddy in that condition. He would say stuff like, "Will you take me back?" I didn't want to say no, because I didn't want to hurt him. I did what I have always done: I kept silent. I slowly faded away from him until he got well. Every now and then the kids would go see him. The kids loved being around their grandparents, especially their granddaddy.

I started enjoying my life again, working and hanging with my friends. Sometimes after work, because that took my mind off a lot of things that I'd been through. I ended up meeting this guy and I dated him for about two years. I didn't trust anybody, but I tried to make it work with him. Months later, I found out that he had a baby on the way. Then he said, "I don't believe it's mine." What a blow to the head! After all the things that I'd been through I wasn't about to go through that again. So I left him but stayed friends.

As you can see, I never gave myself time to find me. I didn't want to be alone. I wanted someone to tell me they loved me and mean it. No lies, no abuse. Just love. And it took me a while to see that unless you have the love of God in you, there is no true love. Nothing but lust.

The bible says in John 3:16, "For God so loved the world, that he gave his only begotten Son; that whosoever believeth in him should not perish but have everlasting life." (That's Love).

7
FOR THE LOVE OF MONEY

Well, as you read on you'll gather that I never gave up on trying relationships. One night I had a dream that my daddy was bringing me buckets of money. My dad was not living at that time. He died in 1985. I got up and began to tell my mother about the dream and she said, "Baby, maybe you are going to be blessed with lots of money." I had the same dream twice that my dad would come with two buckets of money and drop them in front of me and walk off. He never looked up at me.

About four months later, I met this Jamaican guy with lots of money. He started out buying gold, diamonds, furs and giving me money for my children. I said, "Wow, now I can help my mom and my family if they need anything. I have a man with money." So we dated. He was real nice to my children and to me. He put me and my children in a beautiful apartment and furnished it. He bought me a car. I was never in need of anything and I said, "Finally, I met someone who loves me and my children and takes care of me." This was all new to me.

After two years of dating he would say things like, "I used to wipe my ex-wife's 'behind' because she mishandled our child." One night he came home full of blood and the teddy bear that he gave me had blood on it. I said, "What happened?", and he replied, "I took my ex-wife to Parkland, because she needed stitches in her face; I beat her real bad for messing off the money." And I said, "What money? Then he said, "Never mind, you are nothing like her." In my mind I was saying, 'If you do that to me something will happen to you. I will not be abused again.' I laid down and went to sleep.

A few weeks later he came to me and said his ex-wife heard about me and asked him why was he showing me off to his friends. "I guess you think she's too pretty for you to hit and you used me as a punching bag", were his ex-wife's words to him. I asked him if he was still seeing his ex-wife and he said, "No. Only when I take my child money." I asked him, "Why was he telling me all of this?" He said, "Well, I love you, I cherish you, I can't do without you." When he began to use the "L" word I began to consider what he had done to his ex-wife.

One day we were outside playing, we were play-boxing and my mom called me inside the house and said, "Stop playing like that. One day he is going to try you. He looks to be abusive." I said, "Mama, no way." And she said, "Baby, please be careful with him. You have jumped out of the frying pan into the fire", (which means from bad to worse). I said, "Mama, don't say things like that. He's good to me." She still said, "Be careful".

In the month of April, my children wanted to go over to my mom's house, so they did. In that same month was my son's birthday, and on that day my money was kind of low and my car had broken down. I called my boyfriend and he said he was on his way and asked me where was I going. I said, "You know today is my son's birthday." And he said, "Take some money out of the safe and catch a cab." As I was getting dressed and preparing to leave the house, I didn't realize he was in the apartments watching me leave.

I began walking to the bus stop as the cab never showed up. As I was walking, some people that stayed in my mom's apartment complex asked me where I was going and I said to my mom's house. They told me to get in. So I got a ride to my mother's house.

Well, as soon as I got in the house the phone rang and it was my boyfriend. He started cursing in his dialect and asked why didn't I catch the cab and why did l get a ride with someone? I said, "They live over here." Then he said, "I will be over there to get you and it's not going to be nice." I said, "Come on with it brother." I told my mama that l had to leave. I didn't want anybody to see me fight him. My mama said, "That man is going to hurt you." And I said, "That's okay mama. But not here in your house."

My children were watching me. They knew something was wrong. I left them with my mom so they wouldn't see it. I knew if I didn't leave my family was in danger. I knew that he and his friends were dangerous. I have been with them when they jumped on people for different things. So I left. Whatever happens it will be just me and not my children or the rest of my family.

When we got home he began to close up all the blinds in the house. I was ready to fight him back. He made me think that it was nothing, because he knew I was ready. So he caught me off guard and hit me with the back of his fist and knocked me to the floor. Then he began to kick me in my belly and I lost my balance. I asked him, "Why? Why? Why are you doing this? What have I done?" He didn't stop until he thought I was unconscious. Then he took advantage of me in other ways. Later I looked in the mirror and I began to cry. I said to myself, "What have you gotten yourself into girl?"

I waited a while before going around anyone until I had healed. Later my sister came and asked me to go out and he said, "Sure go out and enjoy yourself. Here is some money. Go." And I said, "Okay." I went out and came home from the club around 1:00 a.m. My sister dropped me off and left.

I noticed my house was dark inside and out. I said, "Man... why is it so dark?" I walked upstairs to the third floor where we stayed, got my key out and opened the door. I looked down and all my shoes were lined up. Someone hit me so hard, I almost passed out. It was so dark. I tried to look and see who it was and at the same time a voice spoke: "1:00 o'clock in the morning. Who told you to come in that late?" I knew it was my boyfriend.

I said, "You told me to go out and I left the house at 11:00 p.m. What's wrong with you?" And I began to fight back. It was so dark that I could hardly see him. He pulled all the phone lines out of the wall and continued to beat me, kicking me in my belly until I fell. Then he ripped off my clothes and began to take advantage of me. After he was done, he left the apartment with the door open and I was still laying on the floor hurt.

The next day my two nieces came over and they asked what happened to me and why was I letting him do this to me? I said, "If I leave he will hurt the family." I could not bathe on my own. They had to help me. I was too weak to stand up and my face was so disfigured that I didn't look like myself.

A year later we were taking a trip to New York, my mom said, "Don't think you should go. Something is not right. But I said, "I'm going to a Jamaican dance and going shopping." She said, "I don't think that you should go." But I went anyway.

On our way there, my boyfriend lost control of the car while I was asleep. He yelled out my name. When I awoke, the car was spinning. I heard big trucks hitting their breaks. The car flipped over three times in the air and when it finally stopped I jumped out. But my boyfriend was still inside. I stepped back from the car, because it was smoking. The tires were off -- both front and rear. The car was totaled.

A lady ran up to me and asked who was in the car. I just stood there in shock, so she asked me again. By the time she said it the second time she looked down at me and my clothes had blood on them. My left hand was swollen and my finger was broken. Then she knew that I was in shock. She kept asking me if I was okay and I said, "Yes... I got to get them out of the car." The door was jammed and l couldn't open it. I pulled on my boyfriend and I yelled, "Wake up!" Blood had covered his face. I began to pull on his left arm then I saw it was broken, his bone was sticking out. I still couldn't cry. l looked in the back seat and the guy who rode with us was missing. His shoes were still behind my seat, but he wasn't. His body was thrown out the back windscreen, which had shattered.

The police, ambulance and a helicopter were there. It was a mess. Everything was scattered all over the street: our clothes, etc. One of the policemen signified they'd found the missing backseat passenger from our car and said, "He's not dead. He has a few broken bones, but he is not dead. He needs stitches in his back." My boyfriend needed stitches in his head -- front and back, and I needed work done on my hand.

The police asked me, "What is this in this duct tape?" "I don't know", I said. "I don't know." He said, "Sure you do. It's drugs." And I said, "That's not true. We came for a Jamaican dance and to shop and have fun, not for drugs." He thought I was lying, but I really didn't know. Each police officer questioned us one at a time. We were in Kingston, Tennessee. By this time, I'm really scared: not only did I not know about the drugs, but I'm also out of Texas, away from home and going behind bars. I had never been locked up.

They started reading me my rights. I was crying and said, "I didn't know. Can I please call my sister in Houston?" He said, "Yes." I called her, I was crying and told her that they were sending me away and I didn't know that my boyfriend was transporting drugs and using me to ride with them. I said, "Please call everyone, I'm afraid." They tried to take my picture but I kept turning my head and crying, "No... I didn't know." My boyfriend even said, "She didn't know, please let her go." They made him be quiet and sent us to our cell.

One lady sitting there asked me, "What are you in here for?" I said nothing. She said, "I already know. You all were on the news and in the newspaper. Drug dealers." And I said, "That's a lie." She showed me the paper. There I was on the front page of the Tennessee News with my picture and the name of each one of us. They even had a picture of the drugs. I was so sad. In my mind I was saying, 'I am going to kill myself! Can't take this. Have never been in jail before.'

So later on, we all went to court and the judge asked all of us if we were U.S. citizens and I said yes, they said no. I thought that would help me. The judge asked me, "How did you, being such a young girl, get with these men? And how long have you been with this guy?" I said, "Two years." And he said, "And you didn't know that he was transporting drugs?" I said, "No sir, we always travel but never with drugs. He asked, "How do you know?" And I said, "I just know it".

The judge said, "The sentence for this is ten years" and he sent us back to our cell. I cried and said, "I hate you" to my boyfriend. "Why didn't you tell me what you were doing? I would have stayed at home or traveled by plane, but you used me. I hate you." I said it repeatedly, crying.

A few days later, one of the jailers came and got me out of my cell and let me talk on the phone to my sister in Houston, Texas. I was crying and telling her that they said 10 years and my hand had turned green and I have not been to the doctor. I don't want to be here, I didn't do anything." She said she'd had a talk with the judge and he'd told her he didn't know I had family that cared for me. My sister told the judge that she was my big sister. She explained to the judge, "My little sister just got with the wrong crowd. She has three babies. She is not a bad person at all. Talk to her and you will see."

The judge told her no bond had been set at that time and that he felt sorry for me and hopefully I would learn from this. My sister said, "I believe she has. Please grant her another chance. If she said she didn't know then I believe her." He said there will be another trial next month. I cried and said, "I can't wait that long, I want out now". As I was crying she said, "Baby sis, I'm with you. Don't give up. We are going to get through this okay. Someone must have been praying for me, because I started getting stronger. I began to sing each morning, "The Lord is my shepherd." I could hear everyone saying, "Sing again." So l would sing again.

That month passed and I went back to court. The judge called me up and said, "You know, I didn't think you had any family that cared for you. But your sister called from Houston almost every day asking me to let you go. She said you are a good girl and that you just got with the wrong crowd. I am setting bond for you in the amount of ten thousand dollars." I said, "My family doesn't have money." He said it again, "Ten thousand dollars. That's my judgment. Go back to your cell." I said, 'Lord please help me. My family is not wealthy enough to give up ten thousand dollars. They can hardly make ends meet.

My sister called back and I began to see that God was giving me favor. The jailer came and got me out of my cell and he said, "I'm not supposed to do this, but I know you didn't know any better." He asked, "Why those guys?" He told me to change my friends or next time I might not be so lucky. He said that I'm a beautiful girl but really need to change my friends. He gave me food out of the kitchen and he would let me talk on the telephone to my sister who called me every day. My sister told me that she and her friends would work overtime and I would get out. She said she would talk to the judge again. So I began to feel much better.

The lady that was in the cell with me was a white female who was very nice to me. She knew I couldn't use one of my hands, so she washed my underwear, combed my hair and she didn't let anyone disrespect me. I knew God was working on my behalf. Two months later I went back to court and the judge gave me a lower bail of five thousand dollars. My sister told him to give her a few weeks and she would have the money. I waited to be bailed out. A month later they called me into court and told me bail had been made and I would be released and out on probation in two days. I was so happy. My friend said, "Please don't forget me."

There was a lady coming in who was about eight months pregnant, and she said, "Guess who? I'm not his ex-wife. I *am* his wife and with child. That house you have used to be mine. I had it shut while you all were locked up and the police have boarded it up. Even the cars. So whatever you had, it's no longer there. I have heard so much about you. I told the judge that you knew everything." Then she said, "We will talk again when I get back to Dallas."

"By the way, I have another child with him. Did you know that?" I said, "Yes, I did. But he said you were his 'ex-wife', and that means no longer married." She said, "Every time he was missing, he was home with me. I knew about the time he beat you." When she said that my heart dropped and I walked away hurt. "He called me and was crying and said, 'She's a liar, please don't give up on me'." And I kept on walking. I couldn't believe what I was hearing.

On my way home, on that long bus ride from Tennessee to Dallas, I couldn't wait to see my babies, and my niece that was living with me the whole time I was there. I would dream of my babies... and wake up in jail. That was horrible. But now I was free to see my family again.

Two weeks later, I got a phone call and it was my boyfriend who said he was getting out in a week. He said he was divorcing his wife and I said, "No need, I'm done." Then he started to cry, "No. I can't live without you." He was telling me things he knew I wanted to hear. "I'm sorry, it won't happen again, I love you, I cherish you". He knew I would go for it again.

When he got out we moved into a townhouse: my children, my niece and me. One day he got mad at me and began cursing. He started to hit me again and this time I was ready for him. When he hit me he knew what was about to happen, so he picked up a glass ashtray and threatened to strike me with it and that's what stopped me. That night, after he left, I took my children to my mom's house and I told my niece, "Tonight, I'm going to take him out. I'm tired of him beating me. I'm tired of running from him. I'm taking him out tonight.

I began to throw things I didn't want in the trash. The rest I took back home. He called me to come and pick him up from one of his trips. I told my niece to leave, because if something happened she shouldn't be a part of it. I had it all planned out. He was not going to live any longer. That night I went to pick him up and as soon as I picked him up my headlight went out right in front of the police. The police officer came behind me and pulled me over. My boyfriend was really scared. The police officer said to me, "Miss, step out of the car." And told him, "Stay in the car."

The police officer said, "Listen young lady, I have been taking pictures of this man in the neighborhood and he's a drug dealer. I've been watching you drop him off and pick him up. This man is not only a drug dealer but he has killed some people. I know you are not a part of this; I know there are drugs in this car and this guy is going away for a long time. So forget about him, and whatever this is in the car get rid of it. Then he told me to get back in the car and don't say a word.

I got back in the car and my boyfriend asked, "What did he say?" I said wait and see. I felt so bad; even though I wanted to hurt him, I still felt bad.

He said, "Baby, I'm sick in my stomach... let's go." And I said, "No."

The policeman came back and told him to get out of the car. He handcuffed him and took him away. I cried. Why, I don't know. When I got back to my mom's house she said, "Once again, God removed him from you." I said, "Mama, you know God not only saved him but me too, because I was going to kill him for beating me all the time. God saved me from going to prison. They sent him away for 15 years federal time and he had to do all 15 years. He was sent back to Jamaica after he was released from prison.

Once again, God snatched me out of the hands of the enemy. Psalm 37:40 says, "The Lord helps them and delivers them; he delivers them from the wicked and saves them, because they take refuge in him."

One of the mistakes I made was telling my Jamaican boyfriend the things my ex-husband had done to me. That was a green light for him to think, 'If she let him get away with abuse then why wouldn't she let me? I'm giving her things that he couldn't: money, etc. All I have to do is say, "I'm sorry", with a gift, and she'll forgive me. That's just who she is: a forgiving person.'

Sometimes it's not good to tell what you've been through to another man who's not your husband. Some people will use your past against you, to hurt you. Some to help you. But you must seek God about whom to confide these things to. It could help or hinder your relationship. Always seek the Lord for guidance.

"Ye that love the Lord hate evil: He preserved the souls of his saints: He delivers them out of the hand of the wicked." (Psalm 97:10).

"But the Lord your God ye shall fear; and He shall deliver you out of the hand of all your enemies." (II Kings: 17:39)

8
BACK ON TRACK

I'm getting my life back on track. Me and my children have moved into our new apartment, I'm hanging with my best friend. I was working and doing hair to make money and enjoying my life -- and still making foolish turns in my life. My best friend worked at a halfway house and she introduced me to one of the officers there. She said he was a nice guy. I met him and we were very attracted to one another, a nice looking guy with a suit and tie, a church guy. We talked about the Lord and I said, 'Wow, he's like me... he loves the Lord.' So we talked on the phone day and night, then we started going out.

I would go to his house and he would come to mine and I said to myself, 'This is great. Finally, my life is back on track.' He loved my children, he took a lot of time out with my son; one year turned into two years and everything is still great. One morning I was going to my mom's house driving his car and as I took my exit I noticed a car was trailing me so I kept going. As I pulled into the parking lot, three ladies jumped out of the car and ran toward me and I went ahead and jumped out, too.

The young lady said, "Give me the keys." And I said, "No. Are you crazy? No way." She said, "This is my car." I said, "Lady, are you all right'? This is my boyfriend's car." Then she told me she was his wife. I said, "No way. How is that? Because we have been living together for two years now in the same house. I take him to work and pick him up and he's at home." She said, "Look in the glove compartment. My name is in there. I am his wife. Give me the keys." And again I said, "No. You'll have to get them from him and not me. I don't know you and you don't know me."

The other lady said, "Girl, you are wrong. This is his wife." I was explaining to her that when we met two years ago he didn't have a ring on his finger and how he had spent all of his time with me and my family. He even stayed with my mother. "So how could that be? Let's go to a phone and call him." I didn't allow them to enter my mother's home. So we went to a pay phone and I called him at work. When he answered I said, "Hello. There is this lady here with me that's saying she's your wife?" He said, "Oh, man. Where is she?" I said, "So you're married?" And he told me he was getting a divorce. "I don't want her. Don't give her those keys. The car is in both of our names. I'm divorcing her."

She got on the phone and whatever he said she started crying. I told her I was sorry and she left. I went to my mom's house and called him again and told him, "That's how innocent people get killed. Why not just tell the truth? Suppose she would have walked up and shot me, then what? You would only be sorry and I will be away from my children again, this time for life. When I pick you up go and file (for divorce) or I'm leaving." After I got off the phone with him I started back toward the car, but it was gone. She had it towed.

I couldn't get it. She had every right to do what she did, because they were still married. I called him back and said, "No car. She had it towed. Someone saw the tow truck picking it up." And he said, "You know, it will be right back out." He filed for divorce and we remained together. Now in the back of my mind I was thinking, "Maybe I'm next. What makes me so special? If he didn't tell her, he will do same to me." But I didn't leave. I waited it out. My feelings were too involved to let go.

Another year passed. Everything started looking a little strange to me. I had this feeling that I was being done the same way. So one night he was working an overnight shift and I woke up around 3:00 am. Something said, 'He's having an affair on you.' He got off at 6:00 am.

I went early to pick him up, which I never had before -- so he didn't expect me to be there. As I'm coming off the freeway and making my exit, I can see the job where he worked and there is a lady sitting in the booth with him. She was not one of the workers. When he saw me pull up, he looked like he had seen a ghost. He was afraid so I got out and said, "Hey baby, who is this?" He began to explain. I said, "Get her out". And he said, "No. Because I know you." I said, "Let her out. I'm going to get the both of you. Let her out, I'll be in the car waiting. But I didn't. I left. I just wanted to put a scare in both of them.

He knew I was quick tempered. Even after having gone through so much in my past, he did try me many times thereafter with different women until finally, after four years, I quit. I used to fight him and run after his women friends until one day I said, "You know what? You go your way and I'll go mine." He didn't want it but he had no choice. He was not willing to change.

Sometimes when you go through things in life you feel that you have to settle for whatever a person does to you. My self-esteem had gotten so low through past hurts. I'm a woman that's not only experienced rejection, but constant and various forms of abuse. I was abused constantly by my first husband of ten and a half years. I dated this other guy and his daddy back-tracked after taking his wife to work, came home and raped me. Once my sister's ex-boyfriend also attempted to rape me.

I left a dysfunctional home as a child, from being tampered with by a family member and I couldn't tell Daddy. Why? I didn't want him and my mom to separate because she knew and he didn't. So going through that part of my life caused a major setback for me. I became silent again just like I was in the beginning.

I had no role models, so I began to pray and talk to God. I didn't really understand a lot about the Bible and the promises of God. So I just did what I wanted to and thought that by asking for forgiveness it would be alright in the end. I thought maybe my mom just didn't know either. She did the best she could.

God said to me, "The things you've been through are for a testimony to help others." He said, "I didn't let it overtake you." Sometimes we go through stuff in life because of disobedience or simple ignorance, and as a consequence God has to chastise us like we do our own children. When they get out of line we bring them back to reality.

I thank God because I could have died in the car wreck or through the abuse. But He kept me so that I could be a witness to tell you that *you are somebody and God loves you.* He wants you to give yourself to him, make him your #1 Man. God wants what is best for us because he is our Father. Abuse is not love, it's bondage. It's of Satan. You are God's chosen people. He gave his Son for us to be free from bondage, free and whole so we can praise him freely.

"For whom the Lord loved he corrected; even as a father the son in whom he delighted." (Proverbs 3:12).

"Thou shalt also consider in thine heart, that, as a man chastened his son, so the Lord thy God chasteneth thee. Therefore; thou shalt keep the commandments of the Lord thy God to walk in his ways, and to fear him." (Deuteronomy 8:5-6).

9
WHAT A HAPPY HOME

Two years later, once again, I bounced back and got my life back together: working, coming home to my children and still doing hair on the side for extra money. I was thankful; things were looking up for me. I was able to take care of everything without struggling. I was that person that always had barbecues and fish fries, always serving others.

Every weekend I had something going on at my house. Attendees were mostly family. I would pay for everything: food, drink, even transportation. I'd always been overly giving. My mom used to say, "You let people use you and when you are out they are out." I just love to give out and watch people enjoy themselves. Every time someone would have a birthday, I would give the party and pay for everything.

One weekend my brother's oldest daughter brought her brother-in-law to our barbecue. We never looked at each other in the way of dating, but after all the barbecues and flirting back and forth we ended up talking to each other. At first I was not attracted to him. Why? Because every woman ran in behind him and I just couldn't. So we both just kept laughing and playing with each other. Until it turned into us talking. We started calling each other and meeting each other. Then he said to me after a few of our talks, "I would love for you to meet my mother." I thought, 'Boy, haven't I heard it all'... For guys, they're thinking, 'If I tell her I want her to meet my mother, she'll think I'm really into her.' Little did I know he was for real.

I went to Louisiana to meet his mother and one year later we got married. Two and a half years later, my husband got sick and had to have a major surgery, so we moved in with my mom. I worked part-time and the rest of the time I was being his nurse. The home nurse taught me how to take care of his wounds. My husband was off work 6 to 8 weeks and he didn't like being off work. He was a military man who worked very hard. He took great care of my children and I, and we did not want for anything as long as he was able. He was a great husband and father.

My mother loved him like he was her own son. She said he was the best man I ever had and I told her I agreed. But the fear from my past was still hurting me. Haunting me.

My husband was a very good-looking, well dressed, well-built man and a very hard worker. I lived in constant fear of him being enticed by other women, even though he'd told me I was pretty. Fear was still there from past hurts. For a while I didn't show it, but as the years passed the fear got worse. I had low self-esteem from my past relationships and I didn't give myself time to heal.

When you don't allow God to redirect your life and heal all wounds you will only be taking fear, doubt and all your past hurts into the next relationship.

Finally, my husband went back to work. I would drop him off and keep the car. One day he had me come to his place of work and shop for the kids and myself

This young lady asked me if I needed help and I said, "Not now. But can you go get my husband?" She said, "Sure. Who is he?" And when I said his name she looked very disappointed, like she didn't want to hear that. So I didn't say anything else. I just went on and started shopping, but something just wasn't right. My husband called my name and said, "I'm going to be late; going over to a co-workers house to play pool." And I said, "Okay."

So every week it was something to do with this 'guy' on the job. Now the fear has really come. Again. Going on the basis of this gut feeling. But that wasn't enough to go by. Every week the fear grew and got worse. As I wrestled with this, we were moving into our new home. I tried to ignore it. I prayed and kept on going to church, and he would go too.

We both were strong in the Lord. He got saved four or five months after I did. We got baptized together and I just couldn't believe this was the same man that I married. I was not a nagging wife. I was clean, I cooked, I took care of the home and couldn't understand why this could be happening. I was faithful and when I prayed I said, "Now Lord what is it?" I started getting frustrated. Five years... and now this. I would cry but he didn't know it. I cried to God asking, "Why"?

Then he started taking out of town trips. When I asked him questions he would get mad. So I moved all my things out of the house and he came around later to get them and apologized about what was taking place. And I forgave him. Little did I know he was still doing what he wanted to. Ultimately, he admitted to me that he knew the things he had done -- and was still doing -- were wrong. He said, "You can leave me if you want to." I knew that was a game. He just didn't want to be the one to walk out of the marriage.

I allowed him to get it all out and he said, "You deserve better. You keep forgiving me for all my mess-ups and I just keep taking you for granted. I'm sorry." He cried and I hugged him. But in the back of my mind I was thinking, 'What kind of game is he playing?' Still feeling sorry for him I said to myself, 'God, please help him to be a better man.'

One night I'd gone over to my mom's house. Later, something got me up and I went back home to find he wasn't there. I was driving a rental car, so I sat outside in the car. It was 2:00 a.m. when he pulled up. He was looking all nervous and there was no wedding ring on his finger. He had put it on the other hand. I looked at him and began to cry. I said, "Just what I thought. Game." He said, "What? I went to the movies by myself." "Then where is your wedding band?" He forgot that he had it on the other hand.

He said, "Well, I thought after we talked that night it was all over." I said again, "Just what I said. Game." And I began to cry again. I wanted to hurt him real bad but instead I ripped the curtains off the wall and started tearing things up and he said, "Stop that." I kept right on doing it. He didn't know what was next. I said, "Everything you've done to me will come back on you twice as hard. Someone is going to hurt you just like you hurt me. Much trouble will come to you for how you've mishandled me." And I left, crying.

I said, "God, how can you let this happen to me? I was true to you and my husband. Why would you allow him to do me this way and you do nothing?" Two days later I went back home and he had taken all of his things. I called his job and they said he no longer worked at the store. "He's relocated to Louisiana" they explained, and I began to cry again. I figured he had planned this all along, to leave like that. And I cried myself to sleep. I dreamed he had a little girl that looked just like him. I woke up and I called his mother. She said, "He's asleep. Would you like for me to wake him?" And I said, "Yes."

"Hello, how are you? When were you going to tell me about your move?" He replied, "I knew you didn't want me anymore." Then I said, "Stop right there. No more, okay?" I told him about the dream I had of him having a little girl that looked just like him. He said, "Not me." And I said, "Yes, you." He knew when I dreamed something it was true. So I just said, "One day you will tell me about her."

Boy, was I hurt. Everything in me wanted to give up. So one night I went out with my best friend. I had stopped going to church. I had begun to drink and hang out. I was working as a store manager making good money, just doing my thing. And still hurting. Really bad. Some months later, my oldest sister died of cancer.

I wasn't really mad at God. I just couldn't believe everything was happening to me. Then my nephew drowned. All of this in one year. I called my best friend again and said, "Girl, please pick me up. I need to get out of this house." We went out and started drinking and I began to cry about all the things in my life that I had lost. On my way home, my best friend said, "Girl go home and get some sleep." I said, "I'm not. I'm going to get in my car and go to my house and lay on the floor." She said, "No. Get in the bed, girl. You've had too much to drink."

I got in my car and left. Again, I was crying. I was asking God, "Why? I did everything I knew to do and you allowed all this to happen to me?" I just wanted to die. I felt like I couldn't take any more. I was crying so hard that I almost took my car off the bridge. I passed out and when I came to the car was going in another direction. I almost totaled my car. I ended up having to call for a ride home with my best friend. When I got home both my niece and my brother-in-law asked, "What happened?" I lay in my oldest daughter's lap and cried, "I don't understand. Why?

The next morning my mother was fixing me some food; I had stopped eating. She told my children: "Make sure that your mama eats. She has not been eating." She sent my oldest daughter into the room to turn on the TV to the TBN channel but I said, "No. I don't want to hear it." She turned it on anyway and Juanita Bynum was preaching about "No more sheets." I began to sit up in the bed and listen, tears rolling down my face. I started to repent, asking God to forgive me. And he did. Then all I had left to do was to forgive myself.

The word of God says in Numbers 23:19, "God is not a man, that he should lie, neither the Son of man that he should repent: hath he said and shall he not do it? Or hath he spoken, and shall not make it good?"

In 2 Peter 3:9 we are told: "The Lord is not slack concerning his promise, as some may count slackness but is longsuffering to us-ward."

Again, the Lord said in Psalm 89:34: "My covenant will I not break, nor alter the thing that is gone out of my lips."

God has kept every promise to me. He never said I wouldn't go through stuff. But He has been with me all the time. The trick of the Devil is that he wants you to focus on the problem instead of the promise. If he can keep you distracted with problems you won't be able to communicate with God. Press your way through pain. Pray, pray, pray – or just say Jesus, Jesus, Jesus. Demons fear the name of Jesus.

10
TWO HOURS TO LIVE

"Verily, Verily I say unto you if a man keep my saying, he shall never see death" (John 8:51). I Corinthians 15:55: "O death where is thy sting? O grave where is thy victory?"

In 2000 I remarried the man to whom I'd been married before for five years (then separated when he'd gone back to Louisiana). He did have a little girl as I'd dreamed when we first separated. It hadn't quite felt the same during the three intervening years of our break-up. But I reckoned I'd achieved a lot and wasn't going to go through all of the same things again. We both now worked as store managers and for a while things were going well.

However, despite my optimism for the future I still thought about the agony and pain he'd taken me through the first time. And the more I thought about it the more my renewed trust in him was, again, slowly being eroded. Especially knowing, as I now did, that he'd had a child by another woman during the period we were separated. We went to church only occasionally, and worse: sometimes when I went out I didn't come home; I would stay out for two or three days at a time.

One day we had a big argument. That night I felt like my strength was leaving my body and my daughter said, "Mama, you act like you want to give up on life." And I said, "Baby, I'm sick. I can't help it." The next day I went to work and my steps were getting shorter. I had bad headaches that wouldn't stop. The young lady that was working with me said, "Ms.

Rhonda, are you okay?" I said, "I'll be okay." I started to walk again and I stopped and said, "I need some vitamins. I feel really bad." By that time I couldn't stand up straight. So the young lady rushed me to the hospital.

At first the hospital said they couldn't take me without money and she said, "If something happens to her you will be sued." Then she rushed me to another hospital. They examined me, checked my blood pressure and rushed me to ICU. At that point I was going in and out. The lady that brought me to the hospital said, "Rhonda, who do you want me to call? Your husband?" And I said, "No. We are still mad at each other." I told her to call my mom and my kids.

The doctor said, "We need to do a spinal." And I said, "No. You can take blood or urine. But no spinal tap." The doctor then turned to the young lady that was with me and said she needed to make haste and contact my family, because I was in critical condition. They came in and took blood. I was only semi-conscious, but could hear them talking. They were saying, "This lady is not going to make it. She is going to die. She needs three units of blood. At this point, I heard a man crying. It was my husband. Apparently, he'd gotten wind of where I was and had come.

He said in my ear, "Why didn't you call me?" I was disoriented and shaking like a person who had the palsy. I heard my friend from the Potter's House come in and begin to pray for me. She whispered into my ear the words, "You shall not die, but live and declare the works of the Lord." I now heard my children crying. Looking around I saw my dad who'd been dead since 1985 sitting in a chair in the room.

When I came to myself I was in another room with blood being pumped into my veins. The doctors said it was truly a miracle; they'd given me two hours to live. My daughter said, "Mama, I asked the doctor if I could give blood and he said, 'No. We don't have time; she's going to die'." She said, "Mama, I couldn't take it. I kept hearing you say, 'I have work to do for God. I'm not going anywhere'." My husband told me I kept saying, "I have to sing Sunday." All I know and can recall is what was told to me.

Later when I awoke, my whole family was in the room: my brothers, sisters, children, husband, ex-husband and friends. I heard someone saying that I'd literally died; my lips had been nothing but crust. I believed it because they were still that way. One side of me had been tired of living and gave up. However, the other side couldn't leave my children behind without a mother.

Only God had the right to decide life or death, not me. For seven days they ran tests on me but they couldn't find anything. So I ended up getting out the hospital. I went home two days later, fell sick again and began hemorrhaging and losing blood. So I was rushed back to the hospital and had to have another blood transfusion.

I was kept in one specialized care unit for seven days and then transferred to a different unit where I remained another seven days. I was really sick again and having bad headaches and feeling weak. At that time they ran more tests and I ended up having to go into emergency surgery. I had a large tumor but they had to wait until my body got stronger. They injected me in my belly to stop the bleeding because it had gotten worse. I was also given lots of iron to build up my body for surgery.

Three weeks later I had a 13-hour surgical procedure that removed a tumor the size of a grapefruit. They told my husband that I had to stay in the hospital for ten days due to the surgery so they could keep an eye on me. He took off work and stayed with me, sleeping in the chairs. When I would wake up out of my sleep, he would sometimes be sitting there smiling and looking at me. He would say, "Are you feeling okay?" And I'd say, "Yes." The nurse told me that I could only take bed baths and I did not want to hear that. So I told him to go home and take a shower and relax, I would be okay. He said, "I want to make sure someone is here."

"My sister from Houston will be here", I told him. He wouldn't allow anything or anyone to hurt me. I would tell him, "The nurses made me cry with all those needles." And he would ask them to administer the medication in as consolidated a manner as possible. He also made sure that my IV's were not hurting me.

As soon as he left I got up, pulled a chair close to the bed and I used it for a walker. When my sister and the nurses came in I was in the bathroom wiping myself off and fixing my face and combing my hair. The nurse said, "What are you doing out of bed?" I said, "I can't just lay here. I got to get cleaned up and get out of here." She smiled and said, "All the other women on this floor couldn't do that. You are the first one I have seen do that. It's okay as long as you don't hurt yourself.

I put my house shoes on and I walked slowly. My husband came back inside, smiled and said, "You were determined to get out of that bed." He took me walking up and down the hall and I began to feel a lot better. The next day the doctor came in and asked how l was doing and I said, "Great." And he said, "I heard you were up walking. That's good." He said, "Young lady, you are a miracle. We almost lost you. You don't even look sick." I told him, "I have work to do for God." At that time I was singing for the Potter's House Mass Choir.

As the days passed by, they would check my blood, etc. The nurse told me my doctor was thinking about letting me get out early and I said, "Great." I walked the hall every day to gain back my strength. Eventually, they came to my room and said, "Well you will go home tomorrow and when you get home, no lifting over 10lbs. Just walking and resting. Stay home from work for 90 days. In my mind I was saying, 'I'm going to church!'

A week later I called one of the choir members to pick me up and she said, "Sis., are you supposed to be out?" I said, "Please pick me up because I'm going to praise my way to healing." When I got to church and God said, "Praise your way." I began to lay on the altar during rehearsal. I praised God like I was the only one in the building. When I came to myself God said, "Rapid healing is taking place now." I began to cry and thank God for life, "I shall not die but live and declare the works of my Father."
"I will work while it's day, when night comes no man can work", say's the Lord of Hosts. Each time I went to see my doctor he was so amazed at how rapid my healing was. We serve an awesome God. A healer of mind, body and soul -- our entire being. He is the Great I AM. You fill in the blanks.

I gave my testimony to the choir members one night at choir rehearsal about how the doctors' said I was not going to make it because I didn't have enough oxygen going to my brain and how they called all my family together to let them know that I was in critical condition. I had to give my testimony on how God raised me up off my bed of affliction and how He healed me. God did it and if He did it for me, He'll do the same for you.

A year later, me and my husband whom I married a second time got a divorce. My trust was gone. It was hard for me, even though he was there with me in my time of sickness. But on account of my past hurts from him and my ex-husband. That's why it is very important that you allow yourself time to heal completely from all the hurt because if not, you will only be wearing bandages, and the wounds will still be there covered up. And every time that person or someone new does anything similar to what you just got out of -- your wounds re-open, worse and putrid than before. Sometimes it's a trick from Satan or sometimes it's fear knocking at your door. Again, allow God to heal you so you will know the counterfeit when you see it.

Prayer: "Heal me, Oh Lord, and I shall be healed; save me and I shall be saved, for thou art my praise." (Jeremiah 17:14).

I Peter 3:13 says: "And who is he that will harm you, if ye are eager to do good."

Who wouldn't serve a God like that?

11
ANOINTED AND APPOINTED

Oh, see what the Lord has done in my life! We serve a God that loves even our past. What you have been through. He said, "I'm with you. I'm going to turn your mess into a message. I know right now you want to throw in the towel. Don't, because I have something in store for you. If only you knew it would blow your mind. So now is not the time for you to give up or give in, because the best is yet to come." He said, "Just delight yourself in me and I will give you the desires of your heart. Wait I say on the Lord." Many times we run ahead of God and we think wait means go. Wait means wait, stand still and allow (God) to show you what's yours and ask God to order your steps.

Throughout this book you will see that waiting was hard for me. That's why I was always disappointed. I ran ahead of God. I asked, but I didn't wait.

Another three years passed by and once again I'm living good, working hard and taking care of things. I was working to help out different ministries. Some ministries would still call on me to speak on Mission Sunday. I had different ministries tell me that I was going to be a good teacher some would say Evangelist and some a prophet. Each time I would tell them I like to sing and not preach. I would sing solos when asked.

I remember this one young lady who was an Evangelist and she could really sing. She said to me one day, "Listen, you will be a great speaker. Truth is what people need to hear. Be real and you will bring in many souls for God." I would go out a lot to hear her sing and her husband preach.

She was an awesome woman of God.

In the month of December right before Christmas she died and that took a lot out of me. I had just begun to get real close to her. When she told me I would get married again I said, "No way." She said, "Yes, you are. And I am going to be your wedding planner." Right before she died she knew about a young man I'd been talking to her about. She told me that he and I would get married. She was such a great woman of God. She will always have a place in my heart. A real sister, just real. Her name was Evangelist Kay Shaw and I thank God for allowing me to get back close to her again because true people are hard to find.

The young man that she and I talked about married me on February 14, 2004. We knew each other from years ago. We dated for four years when we were younger. His dad was a Pastor and his whole family was in church. I said to myself, 'This is good for me… his dad has known me since I was a little girl. He knows all about me.' He and my dad both sang together in a group, so in my mind I was saying, 'This is going to be a great marriage.'

The family was happy on both sides. Our wedding day was beautiful, everybody wanted to be a part of it. So we did it: we jumped the broom. After we jumped the broom it seemed like I had jumped past the broom. The word "I do" changed a lot of things. His "I do" turned into "I don't." Oh wow! Now I'm losing it. I don't believe this.

I was working one day and I fell real sick. I woke up in the hospital and my blood pressure was borderline. I was saying to myself, "After all you've been through girl, why'd you get married again?" I kept beating myself up with words, "Now what? This man is never home and we just got married a month ago. What's wrong with me?" I kept saying, "Why can't I say no, to marriage?"

I was a woman that wanted to be settled and happily married. I kept saying to myself, "What's wrong with me? Every man I date wants to marry but after the marriage something happens. What?" I stayed in the marriage. I said I was going to try and make it work. He was so disrespectful to me most of the time and I just remained quiet. I hated to argue and I kept getting sick from stress because I didn't want to be a nagging wife. So I kept silent.

One day I said to him, "Sweetheart, I'm tired of a lot of things and I'm getting ill from being stressed out. I have a problem with you being happy while you are stressing me out. Something has to change. I went back to my doctor and he said, "Ma'am, your blood pressure is staying border line. Do you have children?" And I said, "Yes, I do." He said, "If you don't stop stressing I'm going to put you on some medicine to keep you calm. Paxil." And I said, "Okay."

The doctor told me that whatever it is, I needed to let it go or I would have a stroke. I began to pray on my way home. I said, "God, I'm confused. I don't know what to do. This stress is killing me and I don't want to be out of your will. Father, if I have done anything unpleasing to you, please forgive me. Don't let this stress kill me." I was used to the refrain that I would rehearse to myself, "It's better to marry than to burn." Is that why I married this man? Why do I keep repeating all of this?

I went to my job and told them today was my last day there. That was one of the things that was bothering me. Then I went home and packed up my husband's things and took them to his parent's home, since he said he was there every day. I believed that his clothes needed to be with him. I called the car dealership and told them to come pick up my truck because I couldn't afford to pay for it anymore.

I was getting rid of everything that stressed me out. I put those Paxil pills on my altar and said, "I will not take these pills. It's not my nerves. They're not the problem. It's these things. I began to strip myself of everything and to examine myself day after day. I said, "Lord, have your way in my life. Renew a right spirit within me. If you don't do it, it will not be done. Use me Lord, order my steps. I'll go where you want me to go. I'll do what you want me to do. Use me Lord."

At that point in my life I felt a release in my spirit. I didn't allow anything to stop my praise, not even stress. God had been too good to me. He snatched me out of the devil's hands many times before. He restored my health and my mind. No way was I going to let Satan steal that from me. I said, "God, whatever this is about I still thank you no matter what." I said, "Satan, you should've taken me out when you had the chance, because guess what? I was a fighter in the world and now that I have a God that fights my battles for me you're in even bigger trouble. It's too late! I am a child of the Highest God and no weapon that is formed against me shall be able to prosper." God never said that the weapons wouldn't be fashioned and formed. But He did say that they would not prosper.

One day I stayed home all day, my children were over at their dad's house and I went into a ridiculous praise all by myself. I kept saying, "Yes Lord, wherever, whatever -- I will do it." Be careful when you tell God that.

Be ready for whatever. The next morning I got up. I had enrolled back in school and as I was getting ready that morning for class I heard a loud knock at the door and I asked, "Who is it?" They said, "The police department." I'm thinking, 'Oh Lord, I hope my children are okay?'. So as I approached the door l was afraid to hear bad news. I opened the door and there were three of them who came in. They asked me, "Are you here alone?" And I said, "Yes, what's wrong?"

They ran upstairs and at that point I'm thinking, "Did someone get away from them and they are looking for them?" They came back downstairs out from the bedrooms and the male cop said, "Go and open your back door." I said, "Okay, what's wrong?" I opened the back door and five police officers were armed at my back door. He said, "What's your name?" I replied, "Rhonda." Then he said, "You are under arrest." And I said, "No way, wrong person." He told me to put my hands behind my back, and I said, "For what sir? What have I done?" He tried to explain it to me but I couldn't understand it. The lady cop said, "You can make a phone call if you like." I called my children and told them that the police were in our home and they were taking me to jail and I don't know why.

As they were putting me in handcuffs I heard the Lord say, "Tell me, 'thank you'." I said, "What?" God said, "Tell me, 'thank you'." I said to myself, 'God wants me to say 'thank you', while I'm going to jail." So I began to say, "Thank you, Lord." The police asked, "What did you say?" I said, "Thank you, Lord." They walked me through the apartments in handcuffs, everybody was standing out looking and saying, "That church lady is going to jail. She's always in the house. I wonder what she did?"

As I was riding in the backseat of the police car, I began to ask God again, "What is this all about?" No response. We arrive at the station and they begin to book me, I'm still thinking: "What in the world is going on? Did someone use my name in a crime?" As they put me in the cell with all these women God said, "Tell that young lady over in the corner that she's going home." I said, "What? What about me?" So I told the young lady, "God said you're going home." She started crying and said, "For real? Are you sure?" I said, "Yes, you're going home." Five to ten minutes later and she was walking out the jail just like the Lord said. I turned to Him again, "Lord...?" But He said nothing.

They moved me to another cell and the same thing happened. So a third lady said, "Hey, did He tell you that I was leaving?" I said nothing. I'm like, 'Now wait a minute... what is this?" So they shifted me again. This time they made me put on jail clothes. I said, "Now wait. I'm going home." The jailer said, "Not now, you're not. Strip out of your clothes and put these on." I said, "I will not put that on. I am going home." She said, "You will stay longer if you don't change clothes." So I began to walk to the next cell.

Then God spoke: "You said you would go wherever, do whatever. Now what?" He also took me back to a dream I had about ministering to a lot of women. I dreamed they were on their faces crying out and I stood over them speaking. When that realization hit me I said, "Oh, my God. It has begun here behind bars, the ministry!" I called home and told my family to leave me be, I have work to do for God. There were three young ladies who kept saying to me, "God sent you here for us." Others were gathered around us. I began to tell them all about my past and how God saved me, how He loved them, how He cared about where they were, and how He wanted them to come back to their first love. We had church in that place.

Three of the young ladies said they were "catching chains" (i.e. being transferred, typically, to prison from County jail) the next day. And I said, "No. Not now that you've decided to give God your life. God said you will not be catching chains." One of the ladies asked me if I was an angel. The other one said, "God sent you here for us." One young lady drew me a picture of the ten commandments. The others gave me their information and I said, "You will all hear from me again." God later told me: "Well done, daughter."

At 12:00 midnight they called my name and I went home. The next day I was writing the ladies and the same day I mailed them out. It would only take one day for them to receive their mail. Four days later I got two letters back that they were set free. Look at our God! He is so awesome. Whom the son has made free is free indeed. I began to cry and thank God for using me. God said, "Now you are ready for ministry."

That same year 2005, I was ordained as an Evangelist. To God be the glory for all he has done in my life. I will bless the Lord at all times and his praise shall continually be in my mouth. I cried, "Lord, thank you for choosing me in spite of all my faults. In spite of all the setbacks, past hurts, rapes, abuse, neglect and betrayal. Thank you, Lord. Thank you so much for picking me up. Thank you for cleaning me up. Thank you Lord."

"I've heard people say you are a God of a second chance. But God, you are a God of many chances."

If you haven't received anything from this book, please understand that God loves you and He wants you for who you are. So let go and let God have His way in your life. I'm a walking, talking, teaching, preaching witness that God wants you – just the way you are.

EPILOGUE

Know this, that the same God that made me whole again didn't just stop with me. Today and forever God is healing the sick: the blind see, the lame walk, the deaf hear, the mute speak. Marriages are being healed, families are coming back together. God heals all wounds.

He's the God who heals all wounds...

I am Jehovah-Rohi, your Healer and Mender. My heart is aching to resolve all your problems and take away the bitterness. I want YOU back

...says the Lord...

Don't let bitterness rob you. Past hurts, abuse, drugs, alcohol -- whatever it is. Don't let Satan get the victory. Let's put the devil to flight in Jesus name. Restore!

Every time, I would try but falter in my attempts to write about my childhood experiences: all the wounds, rapes, abusive marriages, abusive relationships, mistakes I've made and different setbacks that occurred.

Until I met this Man.

He spoke to those dead things and said Live!

I know He loves me. He shows it all the time

Even in my pain, my bleeding He loves me with an unconditional love.

He said, "I knew what you would become: a product of Me...
Your Father"...

"The I AM."

He said, "Look at you... you look like me... you talk like me...
The I AM... The Prince of Peace"...

GOD!